SCARY PLACES

Spooky Cemeteries

by Dinah Williams

Consultant: Troy Taylor
President of the American Ghost Society

BEARPORT
PUBLISHING

New York, New York

Credits

Cover and Title Page, © Diane Diederich/istockphoto.com and © Tommy Martin/istockphoto.com; 4–5, © matteo69/iStockphoto; 6, © Eddie Gerald/Alamy; 7, © Mika Semann/vario images GmbH & Co.KG/Alamy; 8L, © Photos 12/Alamy; 8R, © Peter Arnold, Inc./Alamy; 9, Courtesy of Library of Congress Prints and Photographs Division; 10, © Philip Gould/CORBIS; 11T, © Collection of the Louisiana State Museum, Marie Laveau by Franck Schnieder ca 1915 after a painting attributed to George Catlin; 11B, © Leroy Dickson; 12, © Dennie Cody/Taxi/Getty Images; 13L, © MPI/Getty Images; 13R, © North Wind Picture Archives/Alamy; 14, © Time Life Pictures/Mansell/Time Life Pictures/Getty Images; 15T, © The Granger Collection, New York; 15B, © Kenneth Garrett/Danita Delimont/Alamy; 16, © Singapore Paranormal Investigators/SPI.com.sg; 17T, © Photos 12/Alamy; 17B, © ACE STOCK LIMITED/Alamy; 18, © Trinette Reed/SuperStock; 19, © Ghost Research Society; 20, © Abedin Taherkenareh/epa/Corbis; 21, Courtesy of Jason Grunert, Photo by Rachael Plott/I-Mockery; 22, © Ghost Research Society; 23T, © Courtesy of the Chicago Historical Society; 23B, © Courtesy of Library of Congress Prints and Photographs Division; 24, © Scott Speck; 25T, © Bill Ballenberg; 25B, © Marcus Aurelius Root/George Eastman House/Getty Images; 26, © David Crossland/Alamy; 27, © Photos 12/Alamy; 31, © Photos 12/Alamy.

Publisher: Kenn Goin
Editorial Director: Adam Siegel
Creative Director: Spencer Brinker
Design: Dawn Beard Creative
Photo Researcher: James O'Connor

Library of Congress Cataloging-in-Publication Data

Williams, Dinah.
 Spooky cemeteries / by Dinah Williams.
    p. cm. — (Scary places)
 Includes bibliographical references and index.
 ISBN-13: 978-1-59716-562-4 (library binding)
 ISBN-10: 1-59716-562-X (library binding)
 1. Haunted cemeteries—Juvenile literature. I. Title.

BF1474.3.D86 2008
133.1'22—dc22

                              2007031505

For more information, write to Bearport Publishing Company, Inc., 101 Fifth Avenue, Suite 6R, New York, New York, 10003. Printed in the United States of America.

10 9 8 7 6 5 4 3 2 1

Contents

Spooky Cemeteries

Imagine being all alone in a spooky **graveyard** at night. The huge iron gates creak open. The full moon lights a twisted path through the **gravestones**. The shadows seem to grow bigger the farther you get from the entrance. Suddenly, there's a noise.

In that moment, what appears? A ghost rising from a **grave**? A vampire coming to suck your blood? People have reported seeing all that and more in graveyards. In the 11 spooky **cemeteries** in this book, you'll meet a **voodoo** queen, ghosts who won't rest in peace, an ancient mummy, and other creepy creatures of the night.

The Empire of the Dead

Catacombs of Paris, France

What is the spookiest thing about graveyards? For many people, it is the thought of thousands of bodies buried below their feet. Yet what happens when a city runs out of space to bury its dead? In the late 1700s, the people of Paris found out.

Skulls and bones in
the Paris catacombs

The graveyards of Paris had become too crowded. There was no longer room to bury the dead below ground. So people started stacking the **corpses** above ground. They piled them almost ten feet (3 m) high inside the cemetery walls. The weight of the bodies broke through in some places, however. Corpses spilled into the street. The smell of their rotting flesh made people sick.

The government needed a way to solve this problem. So workers moved the corpses to a larger space. It was a huge job. From around 1785 to 1859, about six million bodies from cemeteries all over the city were dug up. They were reburied in ancient underground **quarries** that stretched for more than 180 miles (290 km) below the city. Stacks of skulls and bones still line the walls of these haunted **catacombs**.

Today, thousands of visitors come every year to walk among the long-dead. Many tell of meeting ghostly figures roaming the dark passageways. A few unlucky visitors have gotten hopelessly lost among the bones. These people have never been found. Their bodies now rest forever in the Empire of the Dead.

The Last American Vampire

Chestnut Hill Cemetery, Exeter, Rhode Island

Some people believe cemeteries are home to both the dead and the undead. Vampires are corpses that have come back to life. These undead creatures rise from their graves at night to drink the blood of the living. This practice keeps vampires alive forever, but slowly kills their victims. One man decided to stop a vampire before she killed again.

Female vampire

George Brown felt cursed. In the early 1880s, he watched helplessly as **consumption** killed both his wife and his daughter Mary. Around 1891, his son, Edwin, got the disease. The next year one of George's other daughters, Mercy, also fell ill and died.

After Mercy's funeral, Edwin became weaker. George was frantic not to lose his only son. He began to consider whether there was any truth to the vampire **legend**. Could Mercy have become a vampire? Was she sucking the life out of Edwin?

Desperate, George opened Mercy's **coffin** at Chestnut Hill Cemetery. Though she'd been dead for months, Mercy looked surprisingly the same as when she was alive. Perhaps she really was a vampire.

To end Mercy's power over Edwin, George cut out her heart and burned it. He fed the ashes to his son. Unfortunately, this did not save Edwin. He died, within two months, on May 2, 1892. To this day, Mercy is still considered by many to be the most famous—and last—American vampire.

During the 1800s, one out of four people died from consumption. Like the victim of a vampire attack, a person with consumption becomes pale, stops eating, and wastes away.

The Voodoo Queen of New Orleans

Saint Louis Cemetery No. 1, New Orleans, Louisiana

New Orleans has 42 cemeteries scattered among its homes and businesses. These "cities of the dead" are so crowded that visitors who tour them are warned about getting lost. With the dead possibly outnumbering the living, it's no wonder that New Orleans is considered one of the most haunted places in America.

Marie Laveau's tomb in Saint Louis Cemetery No. 1

Most cemeteries in New Orleans have **tombs** where the dead can be buried above ground. Why? About half of the city is below **sea level**. If coffins were buried in the soggy ground, they would float up out of their graves.

In the 1800s, Marie Laveau was New Orleans's greatest voodoo queen. She produced powerful **charms** and magical **potions**. She held wild services where people were taken over by spirits. She was even said to have saved a man sentenced to death by hanging. According to legend, Marie created a rainstorm that caused the hangman's noose to slip from the doomed man's neck.

Marie Laveau (1794–1881)

Though dead for more than 125 years, Marie can still cast spells according to some people. They say that if you leave gifts and mark Xs on her tomb, she will grant your wish.

Even in death, Marie is still being asked for help. Some say she's still giving it.

A voodoo doll

11

The Ghosts of Gettysburg

Gettysburg National Military Park, Gettysburg, Pennsylvania

A ghost is the spirit of a person who stays on Earth after death. Many ghosts are thought to haunt the place where they died violently or unexpectedly. For that reason, battlefields after a war are often haunted. Yet how does one explain a ghost visiting *during* a battle?

Gettysburg National Military Park

The Battle of Gettysburg was one of the deadliest battles of the U.S. **Civil War** (1861–1865). After three bloody days of fighting in July 1863, around 50,000 soldiers were dead, wounded, or missing. Many were buried right where they fell. No wonder so many ghosts have been seen at this cemetery that was once a battlefield.

One of the most famous ghost sightings at Gettysburg, however, was of someone who had died many years before the famous battle. Soldiers from Maine were on their way to help other Northern soldiers fight the South. They became lost. The ghost of George Washington on a white horse suddenly appeared. He pointed them in the right direction. Some say word of his appearance boosted **morale** so much that it helped the North win the battle.

George Washington

Battle of Gettysburg

George Washington is not the only president whose ghost still haunts this world. The spirit of Abraham Lincoln has been seen a number of times in the White House.

A Mummy's Curse

Tutankhamun's Tomb, Valley of the Kings, Egypt

It is said that people who disturb a **mummy**'s tomb risk death. For more than 100 years, stories have been told of the mummy's curse. Are the legends true? One person didn't find out until it was too late.

In 1922, after five years of searching, Lord Carnarvon and Howard Carter had found it! They had uncovered the tomb of King Tutankhamun.

Howard Carter (left) studying King Tut's coffin

King Tut was a pharaoh who ruled Egypt for only nine short years. He died at the age of 18 around 1322 B.C. At that time, Egyptians believed that a pharaoh's life continued among the gods after death. So the boy-king was buried with everything he might need in the **afterlife**. Treasures included gold-covered chariots, bows and arrows, swords, and King Tut's throne. His tomb remained hidden in the Valley of the Kings for more than 3,000 years.

Lord Carnarvon's discovery of the pharaoh's dazzling treasure made him world-famous. He couldn't believe his luck. Yet less than six months later, Lord Carnarvon was dead. A simple mosquito bite led to **pneumonia**, which killed him. Some were puzzled by his strange death. Was he actually killed by a mummy's curse?

King Tut's coffin

Mummy of King Tut

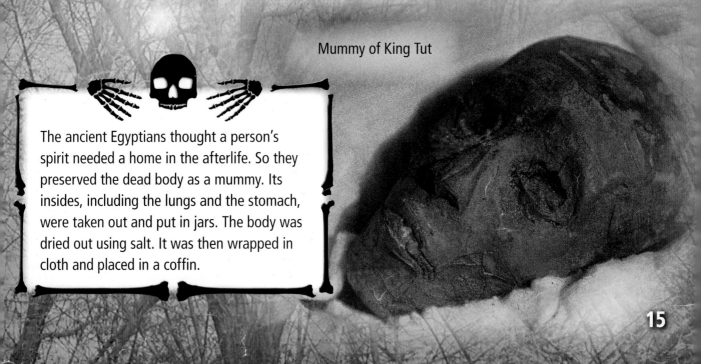

The ancient Egyptians thought a person's spirit needed a home in the afterlife. So they preserved the dead body as a mummy. Its insides, including the lungs and the stomach, were taken out and put in jars. The body was dried out using salt. It was then wrapped in cloth and placed in a coffin.

A Spine-Chilling Spirit

Mount Pleasant Cemetery, Singapore

According to **folklore**, the Pontianak (*pon*-ti-AH-nah) is a vampire who haunts the graveyards of Southeast Asia. It is the angry spirit of a woman who died during childbirth. A Pontianak seeks revenge for her death by terrorizing anyone who comes near.

Mount Pleasant Cemetery

Why is Mount Pleasant Cemetery so horrifying? Is it the thick jungle that blocks out the light? Or the dead bodies buried beneath cracked tombstones? Many feel that what makes the cemetery truly scary is the spine-chilling laugh of a Pontianak.

According to legend, the Mount Pleasant Pontianak is said to disguise herself as a beautiful woman to **lure** men close to her. She then turns into an ugly monster with long teeth and red eyes before killing them. She hides in the tall trees and flies through the air. Don't let her get close! Some people believe she slices her victims open with her razor-sharp fingernails.

Some people think that a Pontianak is nothing more than a large owl. The faces of these birds can look human when they swoop out of the darkness.

Resurrection Mary

Resurrection Cemetery, Justice, Illinois

Ghosts are thought to be spirits that cannot rest in peace. Some mingle with the living for a short time before returning to their graves. People who live near Chicago have been telling stories about one such ghost for more than 75 years.

If a woman in a white dress is **hitchhiking** on Archer Avenue, don't stop the car! Most likely, it's the ghost many call **Resurrection** Mary. She was killed in a car crash around 1930 while hitchhiking home from a night of dancing. Mary has been seen "alive" dozens of times since being buried in Resurrection Cemetery.

One of the most famous sightings happened in 1939. Jerry Palus met Mary at a dance hall. They spent the evening dancing together. Jerry noticed that Mary was strangely cold to the touch. When he drove her home, Mary asked him to stop at Resurrection Cemetery. She said, "Where I'm going, you can't follow." She threw open the car door and ran toward the cemetery. Before reaching the gates, however, she disappeared before Jerry's eyes.

In the 1970s and 1980s, the number of people who claimed to see Mary increased. During this time, Resurrection Cemetery was being **renovated**. Perhaps the people working there disturbed Mary, making her even more restless than ever.

In 1976, a woman wearing a white dress was seen clutching the bars of the gates outside Resurrection Cemetery. Police later found the bars bent. Two small handprints were burned into the metal. Was it Mary trying to get out?

The bent bars of the gate at Resurrection Cemetery

The Hollywood Vampire

Hollywood Cemetery, Richmond, Virginia

Sometimes a person's final resting place is not a graveyard or a cemetery. A tragic accident can suddenly turn a train tunnel into a tomb. Could the fear of being trapped underground turn one man into a monster?

In 1925, the Church Hill train tunnel collapsed below the city of Richmond, Virginia. A crew had been working on the tunnel to make it wider so that larger trains could pass through it. More than 200 people were at work when the tunnel collapsed. Many were able to find safety below ground. There are reports, however, of someone who found another way to stay safe.

Legend says a strange creature clawed his way out of the caved-in tunnel. His mouth was covered with blood. His teeth were jagged, and strips of skin hung from his arms and legs.

The creature ran to nearby Hollywood Cemetery and crawled into a **crypt**. Was it a vampire? Had it been feasting on the bodies of those trapped underground? Or was it just one of the workers who stumbled out of the tunnel with burned skin falling off his body? No one knows for sure.

One statue in Hollywood Cemetery is said to have a life of its own. In the 1800s, a father placed an iron statue of a dog next to his daughter's grave. According to legend, the dog guards the young girl by coming to life and chasing people away from her grave.

The Indian Burial Ground

Robinson Woods Indian Burial Grounds, Chicago, Illinois

When Native American tribes buried their dead, they did not mark the graves with tombstones. With no way of knowing where they are located, skeletons from many tribes have been mistakenly dug up. What do the dead do when disturbed? Haunt the living, of course.

What is an Indian burial ground doing near Chicago's O'Hare airport? When Potawatomi (*pot*-uh-WOT-uh-mee) chief Alexander Robinson lived in this area, a forest covered the land. The Indian chief died in 1872 and was buried near his home. A single stone marks where he was laid to rest.

This stone marks the place where Chief Robinson was buried.

Some say Chief Robinson may not be resting peacefully, however. People report seeing ghosts that look like Native Americans around the burial ground. They also hear voices that seem to come out of thin air. Odd lights have been spotted in the woods by passing motorists.

In 1974 and 1975, researchers recorded the sound of drums beating in the burial ground. Yet there were no Native Americans or drums nearby. Where these sounds came from is still a mystery.

CHIEF ALEXANDER ROBINSON

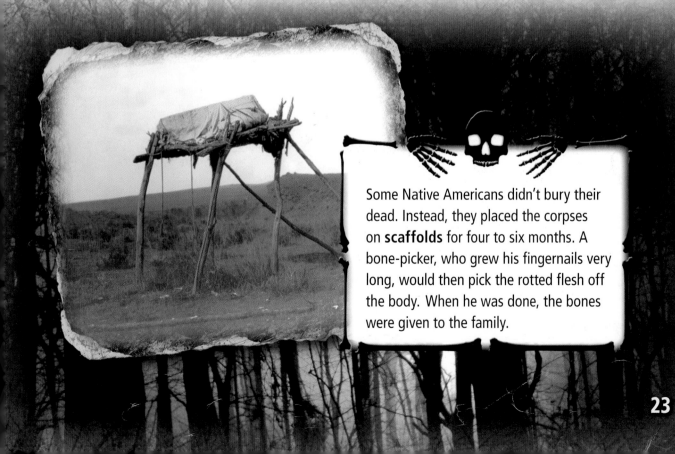

Some Native Americans didn't bury their dead. Instead, they placed the corpses on **scaffolds** for four to six months. A bone-picker, who grew his fingernails very long, would then pick the rotted flesh off the body. When he was done, the bones were given to the family.

Poe's Phantom Visitor

Westminster Burying Grounds, Baltimore, Maryland

Cemeteries are more than just a collection of graves. They are reminders of each person's time on Earth. Some people travel far and wide to pay tribute to their dead heroes. One mysterious stranger not only visits a grave, but also comes bringing gifts.

For more than 150 years, Edgar Allan Poe's tales of horror have terrified readers. Many of his stories deal with death and violence. In 1849, the writer was found lying unconscious in a street in Baltimore, Maryland. He was rushed to a hospital. Less than a week later he died and was buried. No one knows exactly what caused his death.

This tombstone marks the place where Poe was buried in 1849.

Since 1949, a dark figure has haunted Poe's grave. Every year on the author's birthday the stranger appears. The mysterious man is dressed in black and arrives just after midnight. He silently raises a glass in a birthday **toast** to Poe. When he leaves, he places three red roses at Poe's grave. Although he has been photographed, a hat and scarf always hide his face. To this day, no one is sure who he is.

Poe's mysterious visitor

Edgar Allan Poe

One of Edgar Allan Poe's most terrifying tales is "The Tell-Tale Heart." The narrator of the story kills an old man and buries him under the floorboards. When the police come, the murderer imagines that he can still hear the dead man's beating heart. Desperate to make the sound stop, he confesses to the crime.

The Great Vampire Hunt

Highgate Cemetery, London, England

If a vampire is one of the undead, how does a person kill it? Folklore says sunlight will kill a vampire. So will driving a **wooden stake** through its heart, cutting off its head, or burning its body. No matter how you plan to kill a vampire, however, you have to find it first.

What better night for a vampire hunt than Friday the 13th? What better place than Highgate, a spooky, overgrown cemetery?

Highgate Cemetery

In the late 1960s, many people claimed to have seen a mysterious and tall dark figure lurking in the graveyard. Some even said they were attacked by him. Could he be a vampire, as many believed? On the evening of Friday, March 13, 1970, vampire hunters swarmed the graveyard to find out.

A vampire was not found that night, but the hunt continued for years. Tombs were broken open and wooden stakes were thrust through bodies. Corpses unearthed from the cemetery during the hunt have been found throughout the neighborhood. A headless body was even found sitting behind the steering wheel of a car! Some say the vampire has been driven out of Highgate. Yet the eerie sightings continue.

Since Highgate Cemetery was opened in 1839, more than 160,000 people have been buried there. Many horror movies have been filmed in the cemetery, including the classic *Taste the Blood of Dracula* (1970).

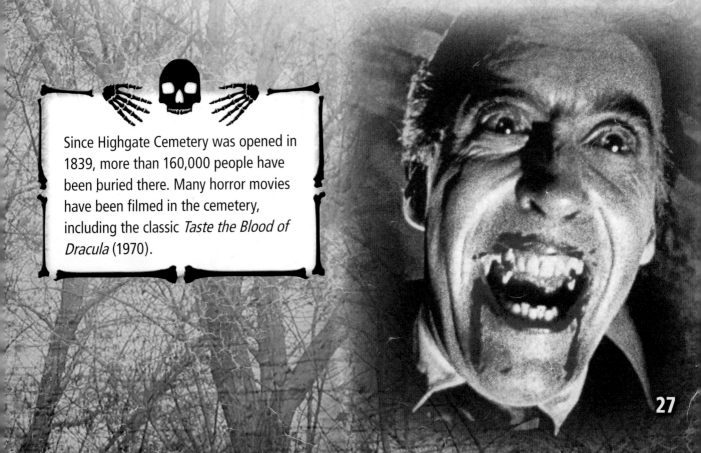

Spooky Cemeteries

Robinson Woods Indian Burial Grounds
Chicago, Illinois

Site of Native American ghostly activity

Chestnut Hill Cemetery
Exeter, Rhode Island

Grave of Mercy Brown, the last American vampire

NORTH AMERICA

Resurrection Cemetery
Justice, Illinois

Home of Resurrection Mary, a hitchhiking ghost

Gettysburg National Military Park
Gettysburg, Pennsylvania

Haunting place of George Washington

Saint Louis Cemetery No. 1
New Orleans, Louisiana

Burial site of voodoo queen Marie Laveau

Westminster Burying Grounds
Baltimore, Maryland

The grave of Edgar Allan Poe

SOUTH AMERICA

Hollywood Cemetery
Richmond, Virginia

The Hollywood vampire

Pacific Ocean

Atlantic Ocean

Around the World

Arctic Ocean

Highgate Cemetery
London, England

Home of the Highgate vampire

EUROPE

ASIA

Catacombs
Paris, France

Home to six million skeletons

Mount Pleasant Cemetery
Singapore

Haunted by an evil Pontianak

AFRICA

Tutankhamun's Tomb
Valley of the Kings, Egypt

A mummy's curse for any grave robbers

Indian Ocean

AUSTRALIA

Southern Ocean

29

ANTARCTICA

Glossary

afterlife (AF-tur-*life*) the life a person has after he or she dies

catacombs (KAT-uh-*kohmz*) underground cemeteries made up of tunnels and rooms

cemeteries (SEM-uh-*ter*-eez) areas of land where dead bodies are buried

charms (CHARMZ) objects that people believe will bring them good luck

Civil War (SIV-il WOR) the U.S. war between the Northern and Southern states that lasted from 1861–1865

coffin (KAWF-in) a container in which a dead person is placed for burying

consumption (kuhn-SUMP-shun) a slow wasting away of the body caused by a disease called tuberculosis

corpses (KORPS-iz) dead bodies

crypt (KRIPT) an underground room used to bury people

folklore (FOHK-*lor*) the traditional beliefs, stories, and customs of a people

grave (GRAYV) a hole dug in the ground where a dead person is buried

gravestones (GRAYV-*stohnz*) carved stones that mark the place where people are buried

graveyard (GRAYV-*yard*) an area of land where dead bodies are buried; a cemetery

hitchhiking (HICH-*hike*-ing) traveling by standing on the side of the road and asking for rides from passing vehicles, usually by sticking out one's thumb

legend (LEJ-uhnd) a story that is handed down from the past that may be based on fact but is not always completely true

lure (LOOR) to tempt someone to come close

morale (muh-RAL) the mental or emotional state of a person or group

mummy (MUH-mee) the preserved body of a dead person

pneumonia (noo-MOH-nyuh) a disease of the lungs that makes it difficult to breathe

potions (POH-shuhns) mixtures of liquids

quarries (KWOR-eez) places in the ground or along the sides of hills from which large rocks are cut

renovated (REN-uh-*vate*-id) improved the condition of something

resurrection (*rez*-uh-REK-shun) a return to life after death

scaffolds (SKAF-uhldz) raised platforms made of wooden planks

sea level (SEE LEV-uhl) the average height of the sea's surface

toast (TOHST) drinking in honor of someone

tombs (TOOMZ) graves, rooms, or buildings in which a dead body is buried

voodoo (VOO-doo) a religion that often involves the use of charms and spells

wooden stake (WUD-uhn STAYK) a piece of wood with a sharp point at one end

Bibliography

Belanger, Jeff, ed. *Encyclopedia of Haunted Places: Ghostly Locales from Around the World.* Franklin Lakes, NJ: New Page Books (2005).

Belanger, Jeff. *The World's Most Haunted Places: From the Secret Files of Ghostvillage.com.* Franklin Lakes, NJ: New Page Books (2004).

Coulombe, Charles A. *Haunted Places in America: A Guide to Spooked and Spooky Public Places in the United States.* Guilford, CT: The Lyons Press (2004).

Hauck, Dennis William. *Haunted Places: The National Directory.* New York: Penguin Books (2002).

Taylor, Troy. *Beyond the Grave: The History of America's Most Haunted Graveyards.* Alton, IL: Whitechapel Productions Press (2001).

Read More

Banks, Cameron. *America's Most Haunted.* New York: Scholastic (2002).

Elfman, Eric. *The Very Scary Almanac.* New York: Random House (1993).

Holub, Joan. *The Haunted States of America.* New York: Aladdin Paperbacks (2001).

Learn More Online

To learn more about spooky cemeteries, visit
www.bearportpublishing.com/ScaryPlaces

Index

About the Author

Dinah Williams is a nonfiction editor and writer who has produced
dozens of books for children. She lives in New Jersey.